Ancient Greece

500 Interesting Facts About Greek History

Table of Contents

Introduction

*Welcome to **the world of ancient Greece!** Spanning millennia, this period of history was marked by incredible achievements in **art, literature, philosophy,** and much more. This book will take you on an exciting journey through time. We explore early **ancient Greece** (c. 8000 BCE–c. 1100 BCE), t**he Greek Dark Ages** (c. 1100 BCE–c. 800 BCE), and further through antiquity until the days of **Greek colonization** (146 BCE).*

*Get ready to uncover forgotten secrets from **the mysterious Greek Dark Ages** and witness how events, like the rise of the polis (or city-state), shaped society for generations to come. Learn about some **key moments in ancient Greek history**, like **the Greco-Persian Wars,** the conquests of **Alexander the Great,** and even battles fought between rival Greek kingdoms and city-states.*

***This book is your gateway into ancient Greece!** Embark with us on this exciting journey through time, where many secrets are waiting for you to discover!*

Early Ancient Greece
(c. 8000 BCE–c. 1100 BCE)

This chapter will explore **the fascinating history of Greece** from **8000 BCE to 1100 BCE**. We'll look at thirty interesting facts about their culture, beliefs, language, and art.

Discover how this ancient civilization utilized nature for food and shelter and developed complex trade networks with other tribes **across the Mediterranean**. Learn about the three main Greek civilizations of the time: **the Minoans, the Cycladic, and the Mycenaeans.**

1. **The Stone Age in Greece** lasted **from about 8000 to 3000 BCE.** People from this period used tools made of stone to hunt animals for food. **They built homes out of mudbricks** or tents out of animal hides.

2. **They grew wheat, barley, olives, grapes, figs, and lentils as crops.** They hunted and fished in nearby rivers or oceans for seafood like grouper and octopus!

3. The people who lived in the later early ancient period in Greece were **the Cycladic, Minoan, and Mycenaean civilizations.**

4. **The Cycladic civilization** is believed to have lasted from **3200 to 1050 BCE, the Minoan from 2700 to 1420 BCE, and the Mycenaean civilization from 1350 to 1200 BCE.**

5. **The Cycladic civilization** was born in the Cyclades Islands to the southwest of Athens.

6. **In around 2000 BCE**, the Cycladic culture began to be overshadowed by the Minoan culture, which began to spread from Crete to other Greek islands.

7. **The Minoan culture** developed on the large island of Crete, which lies about one hundred miles south of mainland Greece.

8. **Of these three civilizations,** the Minoans are believed to have had the most extensive trade routes.

9. **The Minoans** made and traded their wine with many other eastern Mediterranean civilizations.

10. The Minoans had a robust trading system that allowed them to exchange goods with people far from Greece, such as **the Egyptians or Phoenicians.** The Phoenicians are believed to have originated in the area of today's Lebanon.

11. The Mycenean people settled in the eastern part of **the Peloponnese,** the large peninsula that looks almost like an island in southwest Greece.

12. During this time, **the Minoan and Mycenaean kings built large palaces** where they could live with their families.

13. The Mycenaeans were known for their impressive stone walls built around their palaces to protect them from invaders.

14. Ancient Greeks had a rich artistic culture. They created detailed statues and sculptures of gods and heroes in their likeness and painted frescoes on walls inside palaces or temples that **depicted scenes from mythology.**

15. The Cycladic civilization created idols made from marble. One example stands 1.5 meters high and is believed to depict a goddess.

16. Pottery was a popular art form in early ancient Greece. Minoan pottery is characterized by its colorful and intricate designs.

17. Greek sculptures during these early times often depicted gods or heroes made out of bronze. **The famous Mycenaean funeral masks,** which were created between 1650 and 1500 BCE and discovered in 1876, are great examples of early Greek art.

18. Wall art in Minoan ruins shows young men competing in a very dangerous sport called bull-leaping or **bull jumping**. The athlete would leap over the head of a charging bull. In Portuguese bullfighting today, there is a similar contest in which a group of men "catch" a charging bull and see how quickly they can stop it from running.

19. Ancient Greeks also enjoyed playing board games like the game of Petteia, which was similar to checkers and involved two players moving pieces around a square board to capture their opponent's king piece first.

20. **Ancient Greece had its version of sports called pankration.** It was a combat sport where fighters used **wrestling, boxing, and other martial arts techniques** against each other until one person gave up or was knocked out.

21. **Greek musical instruments** included the **lyre** (a stringed instrument), **pan flutes** made of reeds, and **tambourines** made with animal hide stretched over wooden frames. Musicians would often play songs while singing along at festivals or religious ceremonies.

22. **Before writing, people relied on oral storytelling** and songs to pass down information from one generation to another.

23. **The Minoans had a form of writing called Linear A,** which is still being studied by archaeologists and linguists who are trying to decode it!

24. **The Myceneans developed a form of writing called Linear B** around 1400 BCE. Officials and priests mainly used it to keep records about taxes or religious services. **Linear B is older than the Greek alphabet,** which was used during the classical period of Greece (c. 500–323 BCE).

25. **The ancient Greeks were also skilled sailors** who used primitive sailing boats to travel around the Mediterranean and beyond in search of new lands and resources!

26. **Ancient Greece also experienced several wars.** The most famous is probably **the Trojan War,** where the Greeks fought the Trojans for ten years sometime between 1200 and 1100 BCE.

27. **The Greeks believed in many myths about gods, goddesses, monsters, heroes,** and more. These stories were often told through oral storytelling traditions passed down from one generation to another until they were eventually written down into books.

28. **The most famous king from ancient Crete was the legendary King Minos,** who was also believed to be the son of Zeus and the father of the Minotaur. According to legend, **King Minos was the first king of the Minoans.**

29. **The ancient Greeks believed that gods and goddesses were responsible for natural phenomena, such as rain, thunderstorms, and earthquakes.** They even built temples dedicated to these powerful deities so people could give offerings to secure good fortune.

30. **The Myceneans believed in several afterlife realms, such as Elysion** (which the Romans called Elysium), where heroes went after death, **and Tartarus,** where evil souls were sent to suffer eternal punishment. Tartarus was also the name of the early Greek god of the afterlife.

The Dark Ages
(c. 1100–c. 800 BCE)

Explore the fascinating history of **the Greek Dark Ages** in this chapter. We'll look at thirty interesting facts about the culture of this time and the reason Greece entered a period of stagnation and hardship.

Toward the end of the Greek Dark Ages, **the Greeks began to organize themselves into city-states,** cities that governed themselves like nations do today.

31. People call this period **the Greek Dark Ages** rather than just the Dark Ages to distinguish between this time period in Greece and the later European Dark Ages, also called **the Middle Ages.**

32. This was an era when there **were no written records,** so much of what we know about this time comes from archaeological finds.

33. **This period is known as the Greek Dark Ages because there was a relatively sudden collapse of the different Greek cultures.**

34. Some historians believe that a **radical change in climate and bad agricultural practices** that caused erosion contributed to the rise of the Greek Dark Ages.

35. Through archaeology, we know that some communities were completely abandoned for a decade or two during **the Greek Dark Ages.** It is possible diseases, such as the plague, spread through these communities.

36. **The Greek Dark Ages coincided with similar collapses among the Hittites,** who lived in modern-day Turkey. **The Egyptians and the Assyrians were also affected.**

37. Many historians believe that invasions by **groups from the Balkans** and especially a mysterious group known as **the Sea Peoples were largely responsible for the Greek Dark Ages.** The Sea Peoples may have come from the area north of the Black Sea.

38. **During this period, people were focused on survival,** so the use of writing almost entirely stopped. Toward the end of the period, the Greeks began to write again but used letters from the Phoenician alphabet.

39. The Phoenicians were a sea-going people who moved into the area. **Phoenician letters were the basis of the Greek alphabet.**

40. At the beginning of **the Greek Dark Ages,** the advanced palatial estates of the leading Mycenaeans were abandoned or destroyed. Historians are still debating the causes of this.

41. Despite the population decline in Greece, or maybe because of it, **some Greeks settled in Cyprus and even on the coast of modern-day Syria.**

42. Today, the large island of Cyprus is divided by Turkey and the ethnic Greeks. During the Greek Dark Ages, it became a multicultural center with Greeks, Phoenicians, Egyptians, and likely others trading on the island.

43. The island of Euboea, which lies just opposite **Athens,** was the site of a ritual burial found by archaeologists **in 1981**, who dated the **gravesite** to this mysterious era. The burial site included **the graves of a man and woman** who were buried with items from overseas that were **made three hundred or four hundred years before.** Horses with bits in their teeth were sacrificed and accompanied the people into the afterlife.

44. Greece was divided into four main cultures during this time: the Ionians in the east, **the Dorians in the west, the Achaeans in the southwest, and the Aeolians in the northwest, west of present-day Athens.** The Ionians and Dorians are the most widely known.

45. At this time, most Greek people divided themselves into *oikoi,* which were extended family groups.

46. From about **750 to 500 BCE, most Greeks were ruled by monarchs called** *tyrannos* **or "tyrants,"** who held mostly unlimited power.

47. The Age of the Tyrants is directly responsible for the rise of democratic ideas in Greece.

48. During the later part of **the Greek Dark Ages,** many wars broke out between different Greek city-states because of political power struggles among tyrants.

49. Trade between Greeks and the other cultures of the Mediterranean suffered during much of this period.

50. The pottery of the Greek Dark Ages was much more primitive in design than that of earlier Greek civilizations.

51. Even though **the Greek Dark Ages** included economic collapse, war, invasion, and disease, there were still some developments **that would help the later Greek civilization** lead Europe in many areas.

52. **Many early inventions were developed in separate parts of the world at the same time.** For instance, the ancient Greeks developed the water wheel at about the same time it was developed in East Asia.

53. **The new Greek alphabet, which was developed in the mid-to-late 8th century BCE,** spread to other areas of the Mediterranean Basin, especially as the Greek city-states recovered and began to create colonies elsewhere, for instance, on Sicily.

54. **Many people forget that ancient Greeks settled in Sicily and southern Italy,** influencing tribes there, including the Etruscans, who heavily influenced Rome.

55. **Ancient Greeks believed strongly in fate** (a person's unavoidable destiny), which determined events that happened in life. This belief was reflected in literature, such as in the *Iliad* and the *Odyssey*.

56. **Women did not have much power in society during this time,** but they could be priestesses. Priestesses could sometimes become quite influential.

57. **Toward the end of the Greek Dark Ages, in 776 BCE, the first Olympics were held** near the important town of Olympia in southern Greece, where a large temple to the god Zeus was built. Athletes competed in events like running, javelin throwing, and discus throwing.

58. **What large buildings were built during this time seem to be temples.** Like most other ancient people, **the Greeks sought the favor of the gods,** who were thought to grant good fortune to those they favored.

59. **During the Greek Dark Ages, the Greeks experienced a shift away from small villages toward larger cities,** which grew due to increased trade between regions.

60. **Toward the end of the Greek Dark Ages, some cities began to be ruled by a group of the leading men of the city,** replacing the idea of one-man rule and leading to the rise of early democracy.

The Rise of the Polis
(c. 800–c. 600 BCE)

This chapter will explore **the rise of the ancient Greek civilization.** We'll look at thirty interesting facts about their city-states, laws, religion, and trade.

Discover how this period saw significant **advances in philosophy, literature, and democracy** that shaped our modern world.

61. **Polis** is the ancient Greek word for **city-state.**

62. **Around 800 BCE, the rise of the polis began in Greece,** as people started living together in larger communities for protection and economic gain.

63. **By 600 BCE, Athens** had emerged as one of the two most powerful city-states. **Sparta** was the other powerful city-state.

64. However, **there were dozens of city-states**, though some of them were quite small and eventually allied with more powerful cities.

65. It's estimated that **there were over one thousand city-states in ancient Greece** at one time, though the major poleis like **Athens, Sparta, Corinth, and Thebes** dominated their regions and smaller poleis.

66. Though it's often forgotten, **the city-state of Corinth** played a large and important role in ancient Greece. The city lay between the southern isthmus of the **Peloponnese** and mainland Greece. **Corinth's** geographic position made it powerful.

67. **Each polis had its laws and regulations.** In some cities, like Athens, these laws were voted on by citizens who were members of an assembly or council.

68. **Citizens could also participate in political decision-making** by voting at public meetings called agoras.

69. **A vital feature of the polis was citizenship.** Only those born within particular boundaries or who received formal recognition from other citizens could be counted as citizens.

70. **Athenians** believed that all citizens were responsible for participating in public life and maintaining their society's laws **through discussion and debate.**

71. **Democracy developed in some cities**. All citizens could vote on laws rather than having one ruler decide everything.

72. **However, not everyone could become a citizen.** Most people who lived in Athens and a number of other city-states were not citizens. **Women, slaves, and foreigners could not be citizens.**

73. **Citizens were granted certain rights** and duties to uphold for the good of their community.

74. **Citizens of a polis were expected to participate in military activities,** such as defending their city when it was attacked.

75. **The Spartans had a different system. Two kings, each from a powerful family, shared power.** Both kings had to be experienced warriors and military leaders. Sparta developed into a society in which the military was supreme.

76. **The primary duty of women in Sparta was bearing male children for the army.** For many years, people believed that Spartan babies were inspected at birth and killed if there was any sign of weakness, but historians today are beginning to doubt that that happened.

77. **Women in other poleis could own property and conduct business.**

78. **In 272 BCE, there are accounts of Spartan women taking up arms to defend the city** from an assault by the northern **Greek king Pyrrhus.**

79. **Most city-states built defenses around their city** to protect themselves from attacks by rival city-states or foreigners.

80. **Slavery was also common during this period,** with slaves being acquired through war or bought from traders.

81. **Trade between different poleis increased after the end of the Greek Dark Ages.** Merchants exchanged goods for money or bartered items like foodstuffs or livestock on market days, which were held regularly each month.

82. **Currency appeared in the form of coins stamped** with symbols or images representing different poleis.

83. **The rise of the polis** saw the development of infrastructure, such as roads that connected different cities, allowing goods and people to travel more easily between them.

84. **The Greeks developed new and faster ships called biremes and triremes.** Biremes had two sets of oars on each side, and triremes had three. Simple sails were also used, but rowing provided most of the power.

85. **Religion played an important role in people's lives during this period. They celebrated gods, goddesses,** and other mythical figures with festivals throughout the year. They visited temples located inside their cities or sacred sites outside them.

86. **Spartans often spoke of the Athenians as being "womanly" because of their love of poetry, philosophy, and art.** The Athenians believed the Spartans to be barely civilized barbarians with little culture.

87. **Greek theater developed around 700 BCE,** with plays about heroic figures, such as **Hercules,** being performed, usually on important or festive occasions.

88. **The famous smiling and frowning masks sometimes used today to symbolize the theater arts can be linked to this period of Greek history.** Many Greek plays used masks to convey emotion rather than the actor's face.

89. **Aeschylus (c. 525–c. 456 BCE) was a famous Greek writer** of this period. He mostly wrote tragedies, which were quite popular in Greece. Many tragic plays and movies are still written today.

90. **Ancient Greek culture spread across many parts of Europe,** influencing architecture, art styles, language, and literature.

The Archaic Period
(c. 600–c. 500 BCE)

This chapter will explore **the fascinating history of ancient Greek culture during the Archaic period.** We'll look at thirty interesting facts about their **art, architecture, philosophy, and literature.**

Discover how this period provided the foundation for later periods in ancient Greece, including **advances in mathematics and democracy** that we still use today!

91. **The Archaic period was when ancient Greek culture** and civilization began to develop after the Greek Dark Ages, from around 800 to 480 BCE.

92. **The year 480 is when the famous Battle of Thermopylae occurred.** That battle was part of the second Persian invasion, which ended in 479.

93. **Persia was a great kingdom far to the east centered in today's Iran.** The first Persian invasion occurred in 492 BCE. It ended when the Athenian fleet defeated the Persian fleet at Marathon, off the Greek coast.

94. **Even though Athens and the other Greek cities were called city-states, their population was quite small.** Athens probably numbered about fifty thousand Athenians and perhaps twice that number of slaves and non-Athenians.

95. **Not all Athenians lived within the city itself.** There were towns and villages surrounding the city as well.

96. **City-states competed fiercely with their neighbors for power,** resources, and influence.

97. **Cylon of Athens attempted the first known political coup in recorded history** when he attempted to become the tyrant of Athens. This was at a time before Athenian democracy began.

98. **The Greeks developed an early form of representative democracy** (where citizens voted), which eventually became part of many government systems today!

99. **The boule was a body of five hundred men who represented various areas of Athens** and the land around it. Citizens of a certain age would be randomly chosen to serve on the council.

100. Draco was a chief legislator in Archaic Greece. He was perhaps the first to have **Athenian laws written down** in one place for all to see, replacing tradition and the whim of tyrants.

101. Some people resented Draco and his laws. We get the modern word "draconian" from his name. Draconian refers to a law that is thought to be too harsh.

102. Solon was another famous Athenian lawmaker in Archaic Greece. One of the things he did was replace the requirement for holding office from being a noble to just having wealth.

103. Despite the rise of early democratic principles in places like Athens, many city-states were still run by tyrants.

104. The word "gymnasium" is the Latin version of the Greek *gymnasion*. The *gymnasion* was usually an open-air meeting place where athletes would train. **It also served as a community gathering place,** much like today's high school gyms, which hold games and town meetings.

105. Life expectancies were incredibly short in ancient Greece. It's estimated that most people only lived to be between twenty-five and thirty-five.

106. The Archaic period saw a rise in the art of bronze and marble sculptures and pottery painting.

107. Pottery-making became more advanced during this period. Beautiful shapes and scenes from nature and stories based on famous events were depicted. Ancient Greek pottery has helped us learn more about everyday life in Greece.

108. Greek art during this time often featured sculptures that depicted human figures with idealized proportions. These sculptures are known as ***kouroi.***

109. Most *kouroi* are of young men, though some women are depicted.

110. The Greeks developed their own alphabet system based loosely on Egyptian hieroglyphics.

111. The "alphabet" (a Greek word) eventually became the basis of later Western alphabets.

112. Homer's epic poem, the *Iliad*, was written during the Archaic period. It tells the story of the Trojan War and is considered one of the earliest pieces of Western literature.

113. The Archaic period was also a time of significant **advances in science, mathematics, and philosophy.** Some famous thinkers include **Thales,** who is thought to be one of the first men to write down his thoughts on the nature of being. He inspired the more famous **Aristotle, a philosopher, and Pythagoras, a famous mathematician.**

114. Though many earlier cultures used basic geometry, **the Greeks of the Archaic period formed much of the basis of the geometry** we still study in school today.

115. By this time, **the gods and goddesses of ancient Greece** that we know today were well developed. Most Greeks believed in them and their powers.

116. Work on **the famous Parthenon** was begun toward the end of the Archaic period and was built as part of a shrine complex.

117. Today, the Acropolis, the site of the Parthenon, is one of the most visited ancient sites in the world, with perhaps only **the Colosseum in Rome** getting more visitors.

118. Another important temple built in the Archaic period was the Temple of Apollo. You can visit its ruins in Corinth today.

119. By the end of the Archaic period, **there were Greek colonies in Spain, southern France, Italy, Corsica, Sardinia, Sicily, the coast of Egypt,** around the Black Sea, and Asia Minor (today's Turkey).

120. The Archaic period is considered a critical time in history because it formed the foundation for later periods. It was when **ancient Greek civilization** started taking shape!

The Greco-Persian Wars
(c. 500–c. 479 BCE)

This chapter will explore the fascinating history of **the Greco-Persian Wars**. We'll look at thirty interesting facts about how the Greeks and Persians clashed for control, as well as their **strategies** in battle, **key figures**, and events that shaped **this conflict.**

121. **The Greco-Persian Wars** were a series of wars fought between the ancient Greeks and Persians. They lasted from around **500 to 479 BCE.**

122. **The Greco-Persian Wars** were mainly fought over control of **strategic trading routes** through the Mediterranean that connected Asia with Europe. **Greece wanted independence from outside influences.**

123. These wars marked the first time that **individual city-states in Greece united against a common enemy.**

124. **The first Persian invasion began in 492 BCE** and was led by King Darius the Great.

125. **Darius I failed in his invasion** because of strong resistance from **Athenian forces under Miltiades's** leadership. The most famous battle of this period was the **Battle of Marathon, which occurred in 490** and ended the invasion.

126. **King Xerxes** attempted another invasion ten years later but failed when the Athenian naval force defeated his navy at Salamis in 480 BCE.

127. **The Athenian navy was the key to winning battles against Persia's** larger navy due to its use of new tactics such as the **diekplous** and **periplous.** *Diekplous* meant driving a wedge of ships through the enemy formation. *Periplous* meant encircling enemy forces.

128. **The Greeks went on the offensive after Salamis.** In 479 BCE, **Spartan forces stopped an army commanded by Xerxes's general, Mardonius, near Plataea,** which officially ended the second Persian invasion.

129. After defeating the Persian army at Plataea (479 BCE), the Spartans enforced a peace treaty upon them, marking the end of the wars between Greece and Persia until the time of Alexander the Great some 140 years later.

130. Many historians believe that **Darius's and Xerxes's** overconfidence in the number of their troops and ships was partly to blame for their defeat.

131. During these wars, famous figures such as **Themistocles, Xerxes I, Miltiades, Leonidas, and Pausanias** made their mark on history.

132. The major battle sites included **Marathon** (490 BCE), **Thermopylae** (480 BCE), and **Salamis** (480 BCE).

133. The Battle of Marathon is often referred to as one of the greatest battles in history due to its importance in ending **Xerxes's** invasion plans. Many historians believe that if the Persian invasion had succeeded, Greece's role in history would have been limited, at best.

134. Today's marathon races come from the story of Pheidippides, who ran from the Greek coast to Athens to warn the Athenians of the Persian invasion at Marathon. Though **Pheidippides ran over one hundred miles,** the famous marathon races of today are twenty-six miles long.

135. During the second Persian invasion, Greece was saved when **three hundred Spartan soldiers held off an entire Persian army** at Thermopylae for three days before being defeated. This allowed Athens and other Greek cities to form a better defense against the invaders.

136. Today, the famous poem about the **Spartans at Thermopylae** is engraved in a marker at the battle site. The poem was written by **Simonides** (c. 556−c. 468 BCE). The poem ends, "Go tell the Spartans, you who passeth by / That here, obedient to their laws, we lie."

137. The Battle of Thermopylae, which means the **"hot gates,"** was fought near the coast, but today, the battle site is actually a bit farther inland. Geological movements, including earthquakes, have moved the battle site over time.

138. The Greek naval forces at Salamis were outnumbered but used faster ships and superior tactics to defeat the Persians.

139. Athenian strategist Themistocles played an essential role during the second Persian invasion by persuading other city-states to ally with Athens in the struggle against the **Persians at Salamis (480 BCE),** where victory proved decisive in ending the conflict with Greece emerging victorious over Persia once again.

140. The ancient Greek philosopher Herodotus wrote a detailed account of the events before, during, and after the wars known today as *The Histories.* It is one of the most influential books ever written about ancient history.

141. The Spartans were known for their skillful tactics during the Greco-Persian Wars. They used **phalanx formations,** where warriors stood side by side with their shields placed tightly against each other. Their spears, which were different lengths, pointed outward toward enemies.

142. Some **Greek and Persian troops used horse-drawn chariots in battle.**

143. The Greco-Persian Wars led to the rise of the hoplites, helmeted and partially armored Greek soldiers who engaged in close-quarter combat using a long shield and spear. **Hoplites** are an iconic symbol of ancient Greek military might in history books today.

144. After the war, Persian power over the Mediterranean region declined. However, Persia still remained a powerful regional power in the Middle East.

145. Meanwhile, Greece grew more powerful through increased trade with other cultures to become a great civilization by the 4th century BCE.

146. Athens and Sparta emerged as the two dominant Greek city-states during this period.

147. Athenian victories during the war led them to form the Delian League, which served as a defensive alliance against future invasions from Persia or other enemies.

148. The Delian League is one of the first examples of a large defensive alliance in history.

149. The defeat of the Persians allowed the Greeks to make cultural advancements without having to worry about an invasion and ushered in what's known as **the Classical period of ancient Greece.**

150. In conclusion, **the Greco-Persian Wars were a pivotal moment in world history** that shaped modern democracy and set the stage for cultural exchange between the East and the West. The wars also inspired countless works of literature throughout the centuries following it.

The Golden Age of Athens
(c. 479–c. 431 BCE)

This chapter will explore **the Golden Age of Athens,** also known as **the Classical period.** This era saw unprecedented **advances in democracy, literature, art, philosophy, and architecture.**
We'll look at thirty interesting **facts about Greek gods and goddesses and theater.** Discover how this period formed the basis for many modern-day practices, such as **voting** on laws or **electing leaders** to represent citizens.

151. During this time, **the city-state of Athens** became very powerful and influential.

152. **Athenian democracy** was both similar to and different from democracy today. Only male citizens over the age of eighteen could vote. Of the 100,000 citizens of Athens in the 4th century BCE, only about 40,000 could vote.

153. **The Athenian government** in the Golden Age was divided into three sections: **the ekklesia, the boule,** and **the dikasteria.**

154. **The ekklesia** was an assembly of the *demos,* the male citizens. The ekklesia was held about forty times a year.

155. **Any male citizen could speak or bring up an issue in the ekklesia.** Most historians believe that meetings were typically attended by about five thousand men.

156. **Most of the time, the ekklesia was unofficially divided into groups,** with some pushing for one issue and another group for the opposite.

157. **The ekklesia made decisions about foreign policy and war.** It wrote and changed laws and made judgments about public officials' conduct.

158. **The boule was also known as the Council of Five Hundred.** The boule was always in session and oversaw the regular day-to-day operations of Athens, from shipbuilding to diplomacy. **The boule also had the right to choose topics for the next meeting of the ekklesia.**

159. **The men of the boule were not voted for.** They were chosen by a lottery. The lottery system meant that no permanent bureaucracy could establish itself in Athens, limiting corruption in government. Historians have found that the rich and powerful often won these lotteries.

160. **The dikasteria were the courts,** although they operated in a different way than what we're familiar with. **The dikasteria was voted** upon every day out of a pool of male citizens over the age of thirty.

161. **These men would be jurors and judges** on cases from murder to theft. They also acted as defense lawyers and prosecutors.

162. One famous leader during this era was Pericles, who served as an Athenian general for many years. He helped build up the city's infrastructure, including building city walls for protection against enemies.

163. **When Pericles led Athens around 461 BCE,** Athens slowly moved from a democracy to more of an aristocracy.

164. One of **the issues dividing Athenians** during the latter part of the Golden Age **was its relationship with Sparta,** with whom it had allied during the Persian Wars.

165. **Sparta was a military dictatorship. Athens was an early democracy.** Thus, they saw the world in different ways.

166. **Some Athenians believed the Spartans had left them to fight the Persians alone at Marathon.** Other Athenians believed that Athens should have closer ties to Sparta for defensive and economic reasons.

167. **Ancient Athenians** created some fantastic works of art during this era, such as sculptures depicting athletes in marble or bronze, like *Discobolus.*

168. **The Golden Age of Athens** saw the widespread use of architectural styles, such as **Doric and Ionic,** which were used for many public buildings throughout Greece, including **temples dedicated to gods like Zeus or Athena**. These styles are still in use today.

169. **Doric columns** are the most basic of the Greek-style columns. They usually are topped with a scrolled head or a flat one. Ionian columns are a bit more elaborate.

170. **The Parthenon on top of the Acropolis** is one of the best-known monuments of ancient times. It came to symbolize the power and influence of Athens.

171. **Acropolis means "high city"** and was the holiest place to ancient Athenians.

172. **The Parthenon was dedicated to the goddess Athena,** who was believed to protect the city with her wisdom and strength.

173. **In Greek mythology, Athena, goddess of wisdom, and Poseidon, god of the sea,** engaged in a supernatural fight on the top of the Acropolis for the right to name the city below. Athena won, and the name Athens was given to the city.

174. **The patron deity of Athens was Athena,** but city-states had different gods as their patrons. For instance, **the Spartans' patron god was Apollo,** the sun god.

175. **The Golden Age of Athens** saw a rise in literature, with famous authors like **Aeschylus** writing plays about mythological events, such as *Prometheus Bound*, and historians like **Herodotus** documenting wars between different Greek city-states.

176. **Athenian plays were famous.** Playwrights, such as **Sophocles,** wrote tragedies about gods, heroes, and mythological events.

177. **The philosopher Socrates was a well-known figure of the time**. He taught his students to question everything to find out the truth about life and society.

178. **Socrates was eventually forced to commit suicide by political forces** who viewed him as a threat.

179. **During the Golden Age of Athens, women had no rights,** but men could vote on laws if they owned land or were citizens over eighteen years old.

180. **Athenian influence was felt throughout the Greek world.** This included Greece itself, Greek colonies, and nearby cultures nearby, like those in Italy.

The Peloponnesian Wars
(c. 460–c. 404 BCE)

This chapter will explore **the history of the Peloponnesian Wars**, a conflict between **Athens and Sparta** that marked a turning point in ancient Greek civilization. **The First Peloponnesian War began in 460 BCE and ended in 445 BCE.**
The Second Peloponnesian War began in 431 BCE and ended in 404 BCE. We'll look at thirty interesting facts about their alliances, battles, and how they changed life for people living in ancient Greece.

181. **The Peloponnesian War** was a long and extremely significant conflict in ancient Greece. During this time, there were three main powers in Greece: **Athens, Sparta, and Corinth.**

182. **The Peloponnesian isthmus is named for an ancient Greek hero named Pelops.** The name means "island of Pelops," though it's connected to mainland Greece by a strip of land.

183. **The First Peloponnesian War started in 460 BCE** when disagreements between Sparta and Athens over alliances, defensive borders, and cultural differences resulted in open conflict.

184. The rivalry between **Athens** and **Sparta** had been going on for centuries before **the Peloponnesian Wars** began. Many Athenians believed the Spartans were jealous of their riches and influence. Many Spartans believed Athens and its ideas were a threat to the militaristic Spartan way of life.

185. **The Spartans were the strongest city-state in the Peloponnesian League,** an alliance of southern Greek city-states.

186. **Athens was the most powerful of the Delian League**, an alliance that included much of eastern Greece, the islands of the Aegean Sea, and the Greek cities of Asia Minor.

187. Some other important **cities involved in this conflict included Megara, Argos, Thebes, and Elis,** which all sided with either Athens or Sparta at different points during the war.

188. Athens's most powerful ally was Syracuse (in Sicily), while Sparta got help from allies like Persia and Boeotia (an area northwest of Attica).

189. Many of the Greek city-states that went to war with Athens and its **allies were jealous of Athenian power and influence** and wanted it for themselves.

190. Both sides also had mercenaries fighting for them. Some famous ones were the Athenians **Xenophon** and **Thucydides,** the Spartan **Brasidas,** and the Persian **Memnon** of Rhodes.

191. Neither **Peloponnesian War** was fought like the wars of today. At times there were long periods with very few or no battles, but large ones would happen from time to time.

192. Because Greece is a mountainous country surrounded by the sea, **many of the most important battles happened on the water**. One important battle was the Battle of Notium in 406 BCE.

193. Though **Sparta won important battles at sea,** the Athenians dominated the Spartans on the water for most of the war.

194. However, the more crucial battles took place on land, where **the Spartans, through their discipline and tactics, had an advantage,** such as at the Battle of Mantinea.

195. During this time, there were several significant sieges, such as those at **Melos,** which was won by the Athenians, and the long siege of Athens, which finally ended the war.

196. During this time, **a plague killed many people in Athens and Sparta, including Pericles** (c. 495–429 BCE), who led the Athenians during much of the First Peloponnesian War.

197. **In the end, the Spartans eventually won,** thanks to their superior tactics and help from powerful allies like its former enemy Persia and the Greeks in Syracuse.

198. **Persia took over Greek territory** in Asia Minor as a result of their agreement with Sparta.

199. **Lysander** (c. 454–395 BCE) was the king who led Sparta to victory.

200. **The city-states of Thebes and Corinth wished to see Athens destroyed** and its residents enslaved, but the Spartans refused.

201. **Though Sparta had defeated Athens, it respected the Athenians,** particularly their culture and the part Athens played in defeating the Persians years before.

202. **Sparta became a significant power in Greece** for many years afterward until their eventual defeat in 371 BCE at the Battle of Leuctra.

203. **The Peloponnesian War marked the beginning of the end of Athenian power,** though Athens remained a highly influential cultural and learning center.

204. **Alcibiades** was a famous Athenian general and politician who led Athens for much of the last part of the war. After the war was over, he was assassinated while in exile in Asia Minor.

205. **After the war, Athens was ruled by a group called the Thirty Tyrants, which was set up by Sparta.** The group acted as a military dictatorship.

206. **In 404 BCE, Athenian general Thrasybulus** and his followers overthrew the Thirty Tyrants and waged a somewhat successful war against Sparta. They were assisted by some former Spartan allies that were tired of Spartan dominance.

207. **The Peloponnesian War** greatly impacted ancient Greek art and literature. During the time of the Roman Republic, the Peloponnesian Wars were studied with great interest by the Romans.

208. This war was written about by **the famous historian Thucydides** in his book The *History of the Peloponnesian War*, which is still studied today.

209. Military and political history students continue to study **the Peloponnesian Wars.**

210. On March 12th, 1996, **the mayors of Athens and Sparta signed a symbolic peace treaty** with each other exactly 2,500 years after the war ended.

The Rise of Macedon
(c. 500 BCE–c. 336 BCE)

The rise of Macedon is a fascinating chapter in **the history of ancient Greece** that saw one small kingdom expand and become a major power in the Mediterranean world.

This period saw kings, such as **Archelaus I** and **Philip II,** ruling over Macedonia, expanding its borders and building an efficient administration system. Let's explore thirty interesting **facts about how Macedon became a major power player.**

211. **Macedon was an ancient kingdom** located in the northern part of Greece and the Balkan Peninsula.

212. While much of the rest of Greece was engaged in wars with each other, **Macedon became a power in the north,** which was remote and mountainous, making it easier to defend.

213. **Macedon was ruled by a series of kings. King Archelaus I** (r. c. 404–399 BCE) came to power by killing much of his family. However, he is remembered for the many reforms he began.

214. **Macedon's capital city was Aigai** (today's Vergina), where many royal tombs have been discovered. These tombs contain artifacts from the era, such as jewelry, weapons, coins, and pottery pieces depicting images related to gods or heroes from Greek mythology. The most famous tomb is that of **Philip II, Alexander the Great's father.**

215. Under **King Philip II** (r. 359–336 BCE), Macedonia became the leading military power in Greece due to his organizational skills and military reforms.

216. He also created an **elite fighting force called the Companions,** which served as a sort of shock unit, charging into enemy formations and sowing fear.

217. **The Macedonians also developed a unique type of warfare** that exploited their enemies' fear by using large numbers of soldiers in quick assaults. These attacks resulted in overwhelming victories.

218. The Macedonians were equipped much like their southern Greek cousins, but they used many different types of units, such as **heavy infantry, light infantry, archers, and cavalry.** They were very skilled and were able to confuse and weaken their enemies.

219. The Macedonian heavy infantry used a long spear called a sarissa. When used in a phalanx formation, the sarissa allowed them to keep their distance from enemies.

220. The Macedonians made more use of iron in their armor and some weapons than the Greeks.

221. In famous tombs and in contemporary depictions of Alexander, Macedonians are seen wearing pieces of iron armor.

222. The Macedonians also built a navy, which enabled them to establish trade routes in the Mediterranean Sea, thus strengthening their economic power.

223. Macedonia was known for its high-quality white wine produced from vineyards on **Mount Pangeon,** which was popularly exported to other regions like Italy.

224. Macedonia had a well-developed system for collecting taxes and minting coins.

225. King Philip II used diplomacy and military might to achieve his goals and established many alliances with other states, such as Athens and Thebes.

226. Philip II established the city of Philippi near Thrace. He built temples dedicated to gods like Apollo or Artemis throughout his empire.

227. Macedonians also developed their own alphabet based on Greek letters that eventually spread throughout the Mediterranean Sea, parts of Europe, and the Middle East for a short time.

228. Greek culture flourished during this period and influenced Macedon, along with many other regions.

229. Plays written by **Euripides** and sculptures created by **Lysippos** were especially popular.

230. New advances in medicine by **Hippocrates** (the father of modern medicine) occurred around this time. New doctors take **the Hippocratic Oath,** vowing to "first, do no harm."

231. One of **the tombs at Vergina** contained the bones of a woman believed to be a warrior. Some historians believe she might have been one of **the Amazons,** the famous female warriors found in many legends.

232. **Macedonians practiced polygamy**, and Philip was known to have had seven wives. **Alexander the Great's mother was Olympia,** a perfect name for the mother of a conqueror.

233. **Philip II** suffered a wound that resulted in him losing an eye.

234. Generally speaking, Phillip is reported to have been an ugly man, while his son, **Alexander, was exceptionally handsome.**

235. **Philip II was assassinated by his bodyguard Pausanias in 336 BCE,** leaving behind his unfinished plan for conquering Persia.

236. His son, **Alexander III** (better known as **Alexander the Great**), took the throne after Philip's death.

237. **Alexander is considered a military genius.** He was one of the most successful military commanders in history. **His tactics, such as flank attacks or the use of cavalry for surprise assaults, are still studied today by modern-day generals.**

238. **By the end of Philip's life, most of Greece was controlled by Macedonia.**

239. The expansion of **the Macedonian kingdom** was due in part to its efficient administration and strong economy, but **Alexander's** personality made it successful.

240. **The Macedonian Empire** was the largest land empire in the Eurasian landmass west of China.

The Conquests of Alexander the Great
(c. 359–c. 323 BCE)

This chapter will explore **the life, conquests, and legacy of Alexander the Great**. We'll look at thirty interesting facts about **his military strategies, relationships,** and **travels throughout Europe, Asia Minor, and India.** Let us uncover what made this ambitious ruler one of history's most impressive conquerors!

241. **Alexander's father was King Philip II of Macedon,** and his mother was Olympia, a princess from the Epirus region of Greece.

242. **Alexander inherited an army ready for battle when he became king in 336 BCE at only twenty years old.**

243. By all accounts, **Alexander was extremely smart,** incredibly charismatic, and handsome.

244. **Alexander was incredibly brave.** He often fought on the front lines with his soldiers during battles.

245. **In 334 BCE, he crossed into Asia Minor and began conquering lands,** defeating armies more than twice as large as his own along the way.

246. **He is credited for being one of the first to use psychological warfare in battle,** using methods like massing up troops or playing loud music to scare opponents!

247. **After eight years of battles and travels, he held lands in Egypt, Persia, and the borders of India's Punjab region.** Almost no land he traveled through remained unconquered by him.

248. **Before Alexander conquered Egypt, it was controlled by the Persians.** As Alexander moved through the Middle East to Egypt in 332 BCE, many Persian armies fled, fearing they would be cut off from their homeland. The Egyptians welcomed Alexander as a liberator because the Persian rule was so harsh.

249. After conquering Persia, **Alexander declared himself "King of Kings,"** as the Persian emperors did. He also started wearing Persian clothing and adopted some Persian customs.

250. Alexander used to wear a lion's head and skin into battle. It was believed he killed the lion himself!

251. In India, Alexander fought against Porus, one of the most powerful Indian rulers at that time, at **the Battle of the Hydaspes.** Porus challenged Alexander with elephants in battle, but Alexander emerged victorious even though he was outnumbered by thousands!

252. In his fifteen-year military career, which began when he was still a teenager and a prince, **Alexander never lost a battle.**

253. Though Alexander was very successful in battles, it is said that when **he entered Babylon in 331 BCE,** he began to show signs of mental instability.

254. His army conquered many ancient cities, such as Babylon, which was much older than the Greek city-states.

255. Alexander also founded many cities and named them after himself, such as **Alexandria in Egypt.**

256. His beloved horse **Bucephalus** became famous and even had cities named after him in Europe and Asia Minor.

257. Bucephalus and Alexander became the subjects of many paintings during the 18th and 19th centuries.

258. The famous Greek writer Plutarch (46–119 CE) wrote a biography of Alexander, where he says, "When Alexander saw the breadth of his domain, he wept for there were no more worlds to conquer." Though this is probably not true, it's the best-known quote about Alexander.

259. Alexander was the first European ruler to build an army of soldiers from all over the eastern Mediterranean instead of from just one region or culture.

260. His army consisted mainly of Macedonians but also included Greeks, Persians, and Indians, thus creating a multicultural force. No other Eurasian force at the time was quite like his!

261. Because there were so many men from all over Greece and other countries who spoke different dialects and languages, **a new language called "Koine ("common") Greek" was developed.** This language helped people communicate more easily.

262. **Alexander's conquests spread Hellenistic (Greek) culture throughout much of the Middle East, Asia Minor, and North Africa.** We can still see that influence today in architecture and language.

263. **He married two Persian princesses: Roxana and Stateira II.** Roxana had Stateira murdered by having her thrown down a well.

264. **Alexander died at the young age of thirty-two in 323 BCE** after a short illness. Historians still debate the actual cause of his death.

265. Though **Alexander's tomb** and funeral were widely written about, **no one is sure where he was buried.** The archaeologists who find his tomb will be world-famous!

266. **Alexander's legacy can still be felt today**. There are many places named after him, such as Alexandria, Egypt, or Alexandria Boukephala in India (also named for his beloved horse).

267. Alexander is still seen as a role model when it comes to military affairs. **Even Napoleon Bonaparte idolized him.**

268. **After Alexander the Great's death, Antigonus I Monophthalmus took control of Macedonia,** but he was eventually defeated by a coalition led by **Ptolemy** (one of Alexander's former generals). This resulted in the dissolution of the Macedonian Empire shortly afterward.

269. **In 1991, Yugoslavia broke apart**. One part was known as Macedonia, but when the people there declared their name to be **the Republic of Macedonia, the Greeks got upset,** believing they were the heirs to the name Macedonia and the legacy of Alexander the Great.

270. In 2019, they came to an agreement. **Now there is North Macedonia** and the province of Macedonia in Greece.

The Diadochi Wars
(c. 322–c. 275 BCE)

This chapter will explore **the remarkable history of the Diadochi Wars**. We'll look at thirty interesting facts about the battles, leaders, strategies, and consequences of these wars. **Discover how Alexander the Great's generals fought for control** over his vast kingdom after his death in 323 BCE.

271. **Diadochi means something like regional ruler or warlord.**

272. **The Diadochi Wars** were a series of wars fought by **Alexander the Great's generals** from 322 BCE to 275 BCE.

273. **Alexander died without leaving an heir to his throne,** leading some generals to fight for control over his vast empire and its different regions.

274. Although Alexander the Great did not have an heir when he died in 323, **his son with Roxana was born later that same year.** However, **Alexander IV and his mother were poisoned and killed by Cassander.** Alexander IV was about fourteen years old when he died.

275. **General Ptolemy** was one of these influential leaders. He **wanted control over Egypt after Alexander's death.** He eventually became the Egyptian pharaoh, taking the name Ptolemy I Soter. **Soter means savior.**

276. Antipater was another leader whom Alexander had given power while he was away on campaign. **After Alexander's death, Antipater's son, Cassander, became the ruler of Macedonia and much of Greece.**

277. Eventually, other generals, such as **Seleucus I Nicator** (who controlled Syria), **Lysimachus** (Thrace), and **Demetrius I Soter** (Macedonia and central Greece), started fighting each other for their own sphere of influence.

278. One of **Philip II's and Alexander's generals was named Antigonus.** He had one eye. He was a great general, but unfortunately for him, he wanted to rule all of Alexander's empire. **The other Diadochi joined forces against him.**

279. **The Diadochi Wars were fought in various ways.** There were battles, sieges, political intrigues, and shifting alliances between generals to gain power over each other's territory.

280. One of the most famous battles was **the Battle of Ipsus in 301 BCE.** Antigonus I Monophthalmus, who ruled much of Syria, was defeated by an alliance led by Seleucus I Nicator and Lysimachus.

281. Though the numbers are disputed, at least t**wenty thousand men,** perhaps many more, **fought in this battle.** The battle also saw the use of chariots with large knives called scythes on their wheels to cut the enemy down.

282. **In 301 BCE, Demetrius I Soter ceded control of Greece and Macedonia to Cassander,** ending years of war.

283. In 281 BCE, **Ptolemy II** Philadelphus gained control over much of the eastern Mediterranean coast, Egypt, and part of today's Libya.

284. **The Battle of Corupedium** was the last battle between the Diadochi.

285. **By 275 BCE, peace had been achieved** between the members of Alexander's former empire, with each general ruling their own region.

286. The **Ptolemies** ruled Egypt, the **Seleucids** ruled Syria, Macedon and Greece were ruled by **Antipater's** dynasty, and Thrace and Asia Minor were ruled by **Lysimachus.**

287. **The Ptolemy dynasty in Egypt** spoke Greek, including the famous **Cleopatra,** the last of the Ptolemaic rulers of Egypt. Cleopatra was the first Ptolemaic ruler to learn Egyptian.

288. **Seleucus** wanted to rule the Middle East and Europe. Though he was killed before he completed his task, he began a new empire in the Middle East called the **Seleucid Empire,** which lasted from 312 to 63 BCE.

289. **After the death of Alexander the Great** and until the Roman conquest of Egypt, the eastern Mediterranean, Egypt, and parts of the Middle East were dominated by Greek culture. This era is known as the Hellenistic period. Greeks refer to themselves as **Hellenes** and their country as Hellas.

290. New ideas came from the Hellenistic period, such as the **Stoic philosophy,** which would later influence Roman thinkers like **Seneca** and **Emperor Marcus Aurelius.**

291. Some art forms, such as **Greco-Buddhist sculpture**, emerged due to cultural exchanges between Greeks and the people of northern India, who were mostly Buddhist at the time.

292. One of the Seven Wonders of the Ancient World, **the Lighthouse of Alexandria**, was built during this period.

293. **Ptolemy I Soter** and his son, **Ptolemy II Philadelphus,** planned and built the famous Library of Alexandria, where much of the knowledge of the ancient world was collected. Unfortunately, the library was destroyed in a fire that started when **Julius Caesar** attacked Egypt in 48 BCE. It was later rebuilt but was destroyed later on.

294. **The Diadochi Wars** also saw the introduction of a more developed monetary system. Coinage, such as drachmas, tetradrachmas, and staters, were used in trading between different regions and cities, which helped facilitate economic growth during this period.

295. **These wars also affected warfare itself.** For example, Macedonian phalanxes became less common due to their ineffectiveness against cavalry forces. More mobile armies proved more successful than slower-moving formations.

296. One of the most important outcomes of these wars was that they led to a new political system known as a **Hellenistic monarchy,** which provided kings with absolute power over their kingdoms with some limitations.

297. **Greek democracy died during Alexander's time,** and Greece would not be democratic again for over 1,500 years.

298. **The Wars of the Diadochi** proves that when a great and charismatic ruler like Alexander dies, their empire or government often splits into factions. This happened again following the death of **Julius Caesar in Rome.**

299. **The Diadochi Wars** are remembered for their lasting impact on history and culture, marking an essential shift from the Greek rule of city-states into larger nation-states and empires across Europe, Asia Minor, and North Africa.

300. **The decline of Greece and the Diadochi** began when the Romans from the west and the Persians from the east began to invade areas controlled by Greek rulers.

The Rise of the Hellenistic Kingdoms
(c. 275—c. 146 BCE)

This chapter will look into the history and culture of **the Hellenistic kingdoms** that developed after **Alexander the Great died in 323 BCE**. We'll discuss thirty interesting facts about their art, **philosophy,** and how **the Hellenistic culture** spread.

301. **The Hellenistic kingdoms** were a group of kingdoms that developed after the death of Alexander the Great in 323 BCE.

302. They included **Ptolemaic Egypt, Seleucid Syria, Antigonid Macedonia, and Pergamon in Asia Minor** (modern-day Turkey).

303. **These four major powers controlled much of what is now Greece,** Anatolia, and the Near East during a period known as **Hellenic** civilization from about 300 to 150 BCE.

304. The word **"Hellenistic"** comes from the Greek word *Hellazein*, meaning "to speak Greek or identify with the Greeks."

305. At its height, **Alexander's generals** or their families controlled twenty-two separate kingdoms from Greece to the borders of India.

306. **These four significant powers fought against each other** but also formed alliances at times.

307. The most **notable alliance was between Ptolemaic Egypt and Seleucid Syria,** which lasted for almost a century!

308. Around 275 BCE, these **four kingdoms divided up many territories** formerly held by Alexander's empire, such as Thrace, Cilicia, and Cyprus, into various new states. The rulers spoke Greek but had different customs than those of mainland Greece.

309. In some of **the territories conquered by Alexander** on the coast of today's Lebanon and northern Israel, republics replaced kings as the method of governing.

310. This period saw a shift **from an agrarian society** to one more focused **on commerce and trade.**

311. Increased contact between cultures across **the Mediterranean Sea** happened because of improved transportation routes like sea lanes linking the Near East and Egypt with the Greek mainland.

312. **The Hellenistic kingdoms** also saw an influx of immigrants from other parts of the world, including India and Persia. A melting pot society was created because of this. These lands became very different than what had existed **before Alexander's reign.**

313. This period was also a major turning point for religious thought regarding Judaism. **Many Jews began living outside Judea following Alexander's conquests,** leading to reforms within Jewish culture.

314. **This era also marked a major shift from traditional religious practices toward syncretism,** mixing different beliefs into one unified system. The best example of this is how the Greeks and Egyptians adopted certain gods from each other's pantheons.

315. During this time, **the Greek language and culture** spread to places like Egypt, Syria, and Anatolia.

316. **Though the Romans spoke Latin**, much of their culture, especially early in the history of Rome, was highly **influenced by Greece.**

317. Around the time of Alexander's death, **the Romans were gaining control of much of Italy.**

318. **The Hellenistic kingdoms** were responsible for many scientific advances, such as **Euclid's *Elements*,** which laid down mathematical foundations we still use today, or **Archimedes's** studies on hydrostatics.

319. Great works of literature were produced during this period as well. **Comedies and poems** were very popular in **the Hellenistic kingdoms.**

320. **Homer's epic poems** continued to be popular among readers in the Hellenistic kingdoms and beyond!

321. **Epicurus** (341–270 BCE) was a **Greek philosopher** in the Hellenistic period. Though his ideas are complex, he essentially believed that people should try to eliminate worry and anxiety to enjoy life. Today, an "epicurean" usually refers to someone who likes and knows a lot about food, one of life's great pleasures!

322. **Diogenes of Sinope** (d. 323 BCE) was one of history's great philosophers. He built on the work of **Plato and Socrates** and taught his students to distrust what they saw and heard until it was proven to them. This is part of the school of philosophical thought called **"Cynicism."**

323. During this time, **Alexander's successors founded cities like Alexandria in Egypt and Antioch in Syria.** These cities became hubs of learning for mathematics, philosophy, and literature, with famous figures like Euclid, Archimedes, and others teaching there.

324. **The Hellenistic kingdoms** were responsible for many advances in architecture, including building significant monuments, such as the **Colossus of Rhodes**, or intricate temples dedicated to their gods.

325. During this period, great works of art were produced by artists like **Lysippos,** who made marble sculptures, and **Sosos,** who created beautiful mosaics depicting scenes from Greek mythology.

326. **Art during this era became much more realistic** than earlier Greek art styles by depicting people as they looked instead of just symbols or idealized figures.

327. One of the most famous sculptures from this period and of all time is **the *Winged Victory of Samothrace,*** which is on display in the Louvre Museum in Paris. This sculpture was found in Turkey in the ruins of a temple.

328. **Pottery became even more ornate during the Hellenistic period.** It was more flowery and geometric.

329. **The Hellenistic period is the last great era of ancient Greece.** By 146 BCE, Rome had taken over Greece.

330. **Rome took over the last Hellenistic kingdom (Egypt) in 31 BCE.**

Ancient Greek Mythology and Religion

Delve into **the fascinating world of ancient Greek mythology and religion** with this chapter! We will explore twenty interesting facts about ancient Greek gods, goddesses, heroes, and creatures.

331. **The most important god in the Greek pantheon was Zeus.** He was the king of the Gods who lived on **Mount Olympus** with his family. He was also the god of thunder and lightning.

332. His brothers were **Poseidon** (god of the sea) and **Hades** (lord of the underworld).

333. Zeus was married to his sister, **Hera,** who was the goddess of childbirth and marriage.

334. There are twelve main Olympian gods: **Zeus, Hera, Poseidon, Hades, Demeter** (goddess of agriculture), **Athena** (goddess of wisdom), **Apollo** (sun god), **Artemis** (moon goddess), **Hephaestus** (god of blacksmiths), **Ares** (god of war) **Aphrodite** (goddess of love) **Hermes** (the herald of the gods), and **Hestia** (goddess of the home and hearth).

335. Some lists include **Dionysus,** the god of wine and pleasure, instead of **Hestia.**

336. The ancient Greeks believed that **gods and goddesses could affect their lives,** so they would pray to them or make offerings to gain favor from the gods.

337. **Ancient Greeks believed** that their gods were constantly intervening in human affairs, so they built temples to honor and communicate with them through offerings and sacrifices.

338. **The Oracle of Delphi** was a powerful priestess who could answer questions about the future and give prophecies. She was believed to be **possessed by Apollo's spirit** when speaking!

339. The Olympic Games originated as part of religious festivals held to honor **Zeus in Olympia,** Greece, around 776 BCE.

340. Greek mythology is full of **tales** about magical creatures like **centaurs** (half-man, half-horse), cyclopes (one-eyed giants), Gorgons (snake-haired women who could turn a person to stone if they looked into their eyes), and **Sirens** (beautiful women with bird wings who could hypnotize people with their songs).

341. Pegasus is a mythical winged horse that was created when Perseus decapitated **Medusa,** whose hair was made of living snakes. Pegasus emerged from her headless neck!

342. The Minotaur was a creature that had the body of a man and the head of a bull. He lived in an underground labyrinth on Crete where people were sent as sacrifices. The hero **Theseus** killed him.

343. Another interesting myth is about **Pandora.** She was thought to be the first woman created by the gods. When she opened a box she was told not to, all of mankind's woes were unleashed. However, she was able to close the box in time to save hope.

344. In some versions of **Greek myths**, there are three Fates called **Clotho** (who spins the thread), Lachesis (who measures life), and **Atropos** (who cuts the string, causing the person to die). **The Fates** determine how long people will live and what will happen during their lives. Even the gods can't escape their decisions!

345. Ancient Greeks believed Athena was born fully grown and wearing armor. **Zeus gave birth to her**. She emerged from his head!

346. In addition to being the god of the seas, **Poseidon** was also considered the god of horses and freshwater springs, making him exceedingly important in the lives of ancient Greeks.

347. The Trojan War began after **Paris of Troy** abducted **Helen,** the wife of **Menelaus,** King of Sparta. This sparked a ten-year battle between the **Greeks and Trojans**. Historians still debate whether this war took place, but most believe it happened.

348. In mythology, one of the greatest Greek heroes was **Achilles.** He was made invincible when his mother dipped him in magical waters. However, she had to hold his ankle and heel, making that spot vulnerable. **Achilles died in the Trojan War** when someone struck his "Achilles' tendon" at the back of his foot.

349. Heracles, better known by his Latin name, **Hercules,** was known for completing twelve heroic tasks set out by King **Eurystheus,** including slaying monsters like the **Hydra,** the **Nemean** Lion, and **Cerberus.** Cerberus was the three-headed guard dog of the underworld.

350. Ancient Greeks believed in many different underworlds, including **Elysium** for heroes, **Tartarus** for criminals, **Asphodel Meadows** for those who did nothing wrong or particularly great during their lives, and **Hades,** which housed both good souls and evil ones according to how they'd behaved in life.

The Ancient Olympic Games

This chapter will explore **the incredible history of the Olympic Games,** which date back to **776 BCE.** We'll look at twenty interesting facts about the traditions and sports of this famous ceremony of games.

Plus, discover why this ancient tradition was eventually shut down and how long it took before the games started back up again.

351. **The ancient Olympic Games began in 776 BCE** and were held every four years at Olympia, Greece.

352. **Only men could compete in the games.** They had to be free citizens of a Greek city-state or colony.

353. **Women weren't allowed to watch the ancient Olympic Games,** but a separate festival called Heraea was held at Olympia every four years, starting sometime in the 6th century BCE.

354. **During the Olympics, all wars ceased** to allow athletes from all over Greece to participate without fear of being attacked by other armies.

355. **People from all over Greece came to watch the Olympic Games and celebrate in Olympia.** Even slaves were allowed to go, provided their masters agreed.

356. **Chariot racing, the pentathlon, wrestling, boxing, javelin, and discus throwing were some of the most popular sports at the ancient Olympics.** However, when the games first started, it consisted only of running races.

357. **Athletes had to swear an oath** that they would follow all the rules and respect their opponents during the competition.

358. **The ancient Olympics were held in honor of the Greek god Zeus.** Athletes prayed to him before competing.

359. **Athletes wore no clothing when competing.** They oiled up and covered their bodies with sand for protection against sunburns!

360. **Boxers wrapped leather thongs around their hands** instead of gloves like we do today.

361. **Pankration was a combat sport combining wrestling and boxing.** Though it was not the goal, men sometimes died while fighting.

362. During breaks between events, **performers entertained crowds with songs** about Greek gods or heroes from ancient legends.

363. **Cheating was not allowed in the ancient Olympics.** If someone was caught cheating or trying to bribe a judge, the punishment could be very severe. They could be banished from the city-state or receive the death penalty. The Olympics were fun, but they were also very religious.

364. **During competitions, judges used special reeds made of olive wood as markers.** They would break them in two if an athlete broke any rules or did something unfair during the competition.

365. **Winners of each event received a branch made of wild olive leaves,** which was considered a symbol of victory at the time.

366. **Winners also received rewards, such as money, land, fame,** and even statues built in their honor by wealthy Greeks who supported athletic events.

367. **The winners' names were inscribed on stone monuments in front of the Temple of Zeus in Olympia.** These stone slabs still exist today.

368. **In 393 CE, Roman emperor Theodosius I, a Christian, declared banned all pagan festivals, which included the Olympics.** Theodosius ended almost twelve centuries of the Olympic Games!

369. **In 1894, Pierre de Coubertin revived the modern-day Olympics based on ancient Greek traditions** with a mission to promote peace through sports. It had been almost 1,500 years since the last Olympic Games.

370. **Today, every four years, athletes from all over the world come together for the Olympic Games.** They compete against each other in friendly competition, just like their ancestors did thousands of years ago.

Ancient Greek Culture and Society

Explore the vibrant **culture of ancient Greece.** We will delve into twenty fascinating facts about Greek society and culture.

We'll also **discover their love for knowledge, philosophy, art, and architecture** by exploring the stories behind iconic structures such as **the Temple of Zeus** and **the Parthenon in Athens.** Discover what made ancient Greek culture so unique!

371. **Ancient Greek society was divided** into four main social classes: **slaves, non-citizens, women, and citizens.**

372. **Ancient Greek government systems included democracy,** where citizens could participate directly in decisions by voting, **and an oligarchy,** where only a few people ruled with absolute power over all others. These two systems are best symbolized by **Athens,** which had a **democracy,** and **Sparta,** which had an **oligarchy.**

373. **Athenians believed that all citizens had equal rights** regardless of their social class or wealth. This concept is called "equality before the law" today.

374. **Ancient Greeks believed in many gods** who they sometimes worshiped through festivals. **The Panathenea** was an Athenian religious festival that was held every four years.

375. **The stories of the gods helped the Greeks make sense of their world.** We call them myths, but to the Greeks, they were true.

376. **The Greeks developed their alphabet from the Phoenicians.** The English word "alphabet" comes from the first two letters of the Greek alphabet, "alpha" and "beta."

377. **Theater was very popular in ancient Greece**. It was used as a form of entertainment and a way to educate people about morality and politics.

378. **Ancient Greeks developed advanced mathematics and philosophies** to explain the world around them.

379. **Ancient Athenians believed that education led to success,** so they developed an education system where children were taught reading, writing, mathematics, and philosophy.

380. **Archimedes** (c. 287–212 BCE) developed the water screw, which could move water from a lower level to a higher level, making labor easier.

381. Ancient Greece gave birth to many famous writers and philosophers, such as **Homer, Socrates, Aristotle, and Plato.**

382. **The Greek philosopher Plato wrote about ideas like justice, beauty, and truth.** Plato's teachings are still taught in many countries today.

383. **Ancient Greeks created sculptures from marble or bronze depicting gods, heroes, and everyday life.** These pieces of art are still admired today.

384. **Vase painting was an important art form in ancient Greece.** Vases depicted scenes from everyday life or mythology and often used bright colors like reds, blues, and yellows.

385. One of the Seven Wonders of the Ancient World was **the Colossus of Rhodes,** a giant statue. The giant's feet are said to have stood on opposite sides of the harbor entrance of Rhodes. The statue stood over one hundred feet high!

386. **Ancient Greeks believed that music had healing powers,** so they played flutes and lyres for this purpose. Some even used these instruments during battles.

387. **Ancient Greek architecture is known for its grand columns and the temples built to honor gods.**

388. **The Temple of Zeus,** one of the most important temples in ancient Greece, can be seen in Athens. It is not far from the Acropolis.

389. **The Parthenon in Athens was a building dedicated to the goddess Athena**. It housed sculptures and paintings depicting gods and heroes from Greek mythology.

390. In Centennial Park in Nashville, Tennessee, you can find a full-sized replica of the **Parthenon,** including a **statue of Athena** inside. Historians and archaeologists believe the replica is accurate.

Ancient Greek Philosophy

This chapter will explore the fascinating **history of ancient Greek philosophy,** a tradition that dates back to **Thales.**
We'll look at twenty interesting facts about the works and beliefs of some of the most influential thinkers in history, such as **Plato, Aristotle, Epicurus, and Socrates.** Discover how these philosophers changed our understanding of knowledge and created ideas that are still relevant today!

391. Many historians believe **ancient Greek philosophy began over 2,500 years ago with the philosopher Thales.** Many modern scientific and philosophical ideas are rooted in ancient Greek thought.

392. The first great philosophers were called the Pre-Socratics because they came before **the great philosopher Socrates (c. 469–399 BCE).**

393. **Socrates developed the Socratic method to encourage people to think** for themselves and ask questions rather than accept something just because it was what they were taught.

394. **Socrates was eventually forced to commit suicide** by men who were overthrowing Athenian democracy. They wanted him to stop asking questions and teaching young people to do the same.

395. **Plato was a student of Socrates and created his school of philosophy, the Academy, in Athens.** The Academy existed from 387 to 86 BCE, when it was destroyed by the Romans.

396. **Plato's most famous book is called the *Republic*.** In it, he argues that certain people are best suited for certain jobs. **The *Republic* represented an ideal,** but it is widely criticized today for placing some types of people above others.

397. Aristotle, another famous philosopher, was a **student at Plato's Academy.** Aristotle made several important contributions to fields like biology, ethics, and politics.

398. Later in life, **Aristotle started his own school called the Lyceum.** The French word *lycee*, which means high-school-aged students, comes directly from ancient Greece.

399. Aristotle wrote several important works, including *Metaphysics,* which discusses the nature of reality, *Nicomachean Ethics* on ethical behavior, and *Politics* about how societies would best work.

400. Heraclitus was an early Greek philosopher who argued that **everything is connected** and that **everything is constantly changing.** He believed people should try to live with this idea in mind.

401. Parmenides believed that there were **two sides to reality:** things as they really are and how a person believes them to be.

402. Zeno of Elea developed **paradoxes** that challenged our understanding by presenting illogical or impossible ideas that were still true.

403. Epicurus was one of the most influential thinkers on **hedonism** (seeking pleasure as a way to live a happy life). Today, someone who enjoys good food and wine is sometimes called an epicure.

404. The **Cynics** rejected material possessions and any status or power, believing that true happiness came from living simply.

405. Stoicism was another belief system of ancient Greece and, later, Rome. The Stoics believed that balance in all things led to a healthy mind and spirit.

406. The Sophists were teachers who taught their students rhetoric **(the art of persuasion)** and logic. Philosophical education was considered very important to the Athenians and some of the other Greeks, especially among the elite.

407. Protagoras was one of the most famous Sophists. He wrote, **"Man is the measure of all things,"** meaning everyone has their own truth.

408. Democritus developed early **atomic theory.** The Atomists believed that everything was made up of tiny indivisible particles called atoms.

409. Pythagoras developed a **mathematical theory about the solar system,** stating that the planets moved according to mathematical principles, which they do. He thought that since math was the root of music, the planets must create a type of music of their own.

410. The richest and most powerful families of the Roman Empire often hired Greek tutors for their children. Greeks were considered the most educated people in the known world by the Romans, even long after the glory of Greece was in the past.

Ancient Greek Mathematics

This chapter will explore **the fascinating history of mathematics in ancient Greece** and reveal twenty interesting facts about mathematical discoveries and theories.
We'll look at some of the most influential mathematicians, such as Thales, **Euclid,** and **Pythagoras,** who laid down **the roots for geometry** that we still use today!

411. Ancient Greeks were the first people to create an organized written system of mathematics.

412. The Babylonians passed down knowledge of astronomy and mathematical methods to the ancient Greeks, who built on them, allowing for a more advanced understanding of concepts such as calendars and timekeeping systems.

413. The famous mathematician Thales lived around 600 BCE. He used an early geometric theorem called Thales's theorem, which might be the first mathematical rule ever discovered.

414. Pythagoras was another influential figure from ancient Greece who theorized that numbers could explain everything and created what we now call the **Pythagorean theorem ($A^2 + B^2 = C^2$).**

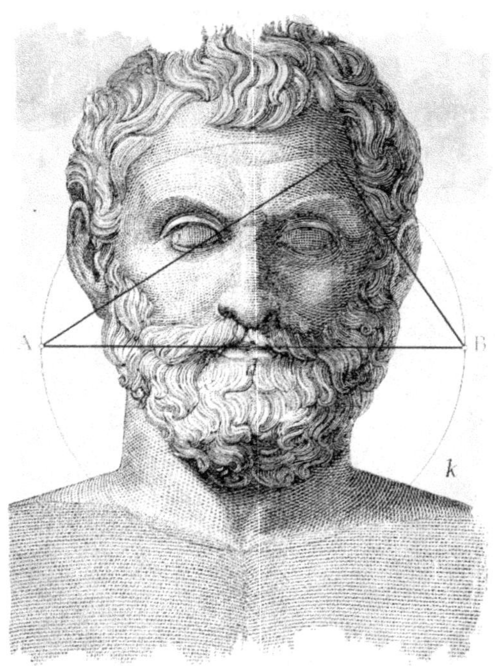

415. Hippias of Elis discovered the **quadratrix,** the way in which certain types of curves occur in nature. This was an early discovery in the field of physics.

416. Zeno's paradoxes challenged conventional thinking about space, time, and motion by posing questions like Achilles' paradox: How can Achilles ever outrun the tortoise if at every moment they are always separated? This paradox was solved using mathematics.

417. Aristotle's work on logic set up foundations for mathematical reasoning still used today. He wrote extensively about how logical arguments can lead us closer to truth or understanding complex issues better than just relying on empiricism (knowledge through personal experience) alone.

418. Euclid wrote *Elements*, which is considered one of the most influential works in mathematical history during Greece's Golden Age in the 3rd century BCE.

419. **Euclidean geometry** is named after him and has been studied for generations. **Euclid is considered to be the father of geometry.**

420. **Archimedes** used math to build machines like levers and pulleys for lifting heavy objects without using brute force or muscle power.

421. He also invented many other machines, such as a weapon called **the claw, which could hook enemy ships** approaching the shore.

422. **Pappus wrote the *Collection*,** which is considered one of the most important works from ancient Greece. It includes many mathematical topics, such as projective and Euclidean geometry.

423. **Pappus** also invented what we now call **Pascal's triangle.**

424. **Archimedes** developed methods for **calculating pi (π),** which we still use today.

425. **Eratosthenes** was an ancient Greek mathematician and chief librarian at **the Library of Alexandria.** He calculated the circumference of the Earth using geometry principles. It was only off by about 15 percent!

426. **Diophantus** created **algebraic methods** that are used today to solve complex equations. These methods were included in his famous book collection ***Arithmetica,*** which contains hundreds of problems and their solutions.

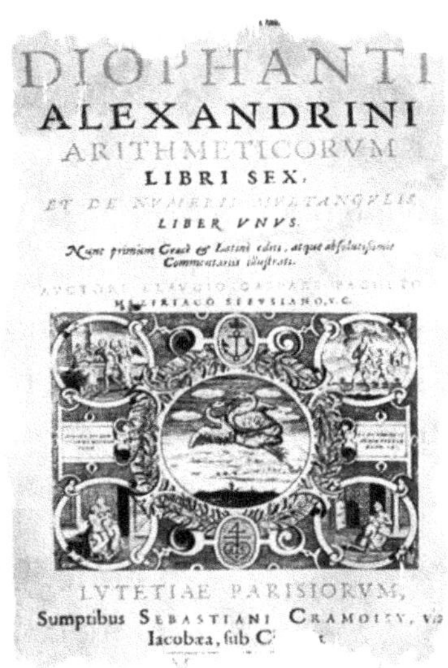

427. **Apollonius's** work on conic sections revolutionized geometry by introducing new shapes and advancing both math and geometry.

428. **The Greeks discovered algebraic equations** and used them to solve everyday problems.

429. **The ancient Greeks** were the first to use letters of the alphabet as symbols for unknown numbers in equations, a method we still use today.

430. **Ancient Greeks used geometric principles to design buildings** with proportions pleasing to the eye. Some examples include the **Parthenon in Athens**, which was built around 438 BCE, and **the Temple of Zeus at Olympia,** which was built around 463 BCE.

Ancient Greek Science and Technology

This chapter will explore the incredible advances in **science and technology achieved by the ancient Greeks.** We'll look at twenty interesting facts about their inventions and discoveries, some of which were used for centuries.

From **the first computer to early robots,** we'll discover how the Greeks laid the foundations for modern-day scientific thought!

431. The ancient Greeks invented the rudimentary analog computer (a computer being a device that can provide answers)!

432. This computer was **Antikythera Mechanism**, an ancient Greek astronomical device that used gears and dials to predict celestial events like eclipses during the 2nd century BCE. It was rediscovered in 1901 CE!

433. Ancient Greeks also developed some basic early forms of robotics, like the gear-powered servant of **Philon,** which could pour a person a glass of wine.

434. The Greeks were also the first to accurately measure time with a sundial that divided the day into twelve equal parts of daylight and nighttime hours. **Aristarchus** of Samos is thought to be its inventor.

435. Like other ancient cultures, the ancient Greeks developed aqueducts that **used gravity to transport water from mountains** or hills into cities for drinking, washing, and bathing purposes.

436. Ancient Greek scientists were the first in history to use **mathematics** as a way of understanding nature around them. This led to advances in physics, astronomy, and engineering.

437. The ancient Greeks used a form of geometry called triangulation to measure distances in the open sea. This was an essential way for them to navigate unknown waters and find new places.

438. Hipparchus (190–120 BCE) laid the foundations of what would become **trigonometry,** making it possible for people to calculate angles and distances between objects using circles and triangles. These principles are still used by astronomers when they measure stars or galaxies.

439. **Eratosthenes** (276-194 BCE) calculated the circumference of the Earth by measuring shadows at two locations during midday on the summer solstice, concluding that Earth must be round if both measurements matched up correctly.

440. **The mathematician Pythagoras** (570–495 BCE) discovered the famous theorem bearing his name after experimenting with triangles. Scientists today still use his work to make calculations.

441. **The mathematician Thales** (624–546 BCE) studied electricity by experimenting with amber stones.

442. **The philosopher Anaximander** (610–546 BCE) created maps by measuring distances between cities and plotting them on paper. This was one of the earliest examples of cartography.

443. In 490 BCE, **Hippocrates** founded medical science by separating medicine from superstition.

444. **Hippocrates** is known as the father of modern medicine for his contributions, which **included clinical observation** and diagnosis using natural remedies rather than magic or religion-based treatments.

445. **The scientist Herophilus** (335–280 BCE) conducted groundbreaking research into human **anatomy,** like discovering the function of certain nerves and distinguishing arteries from veins.

446. **Archimedes** is credited with inventing a **primitive odometer**, which allowed Greek generals to know how far they had traveled.

447. **Aristotle developed a theory of motion** that provided a basic understanding of motion until **Isaac Newton's** groundbreaking discovery of the actual laws of motion.

448. **Aristotle's** work also included **taxonomy** or **classification systems** for living things, which scientists still use today **to categorize species** based on their characteristics.

449. **The Greeks** were the first to identify planets in the sky. Five are visible to the naked eye: **Hermes, Aphrodite, Ares, Zeus, and Cronus.** We know them by the names the Romans gave them: Mercury, Venus, Mars, Jupiter, and Saturn.

450. **Modern scientists gave names to constellations based on Greek and Roman myths.** One of the most recognizable is **Orion,** the name of a mythological Greek hunter.

Ancient Greek Art and Architecture

This chapter will explore ten facts about **ancient Greek art and architecture.** We'll discover how they used symmetry to build iconic structures like **the Parthenon,** as well as their **beautiful sculptures and paintings.**

451. What we recognize as **ancient Greek art and architecture** began around 900 BCE. Many of the designs used in ancient Greek art are still seen today, such as columns, statues, and friezes **(ornamental sculptures).**

452. **Architecture during this period** focused heavily on **symmetry and balance,** which can be seen through the use of columns and triangular pediments (the triangular top of the end of the roof) on important buildings like temples.

453. **Architecture in ancient Greece** featured three main styles: **Doric** (simplest), **Ionic** (more ornate), and **Corinthian** (most intricate).

454. **The Parthenon is the most famous example** of ancient Greek architecture. This temple was built in Athens on the Acropolis, a hill, between 447 and 438 BCE!

455. **The Greeks used mosaics to decorate** floors, walls, and ceilings. Mosaics can still be seen in archaeological sites across Greece.

456. **Paintings usually depicted scenes from mythology.** Painting could be found on vases or other objects. They could also be on walls or ceilings inside temples and other buildings.

457. **Pottery** was one of the earliest forms of ancient Greek artwork. **Painted vases** were often created to be buried with people when they died for them to use in the afterlife.

458. **Sculptures in bronze or marble were popular too.** Some famous examples include *Athena Parthenos* by Phidias and the *Discobolus* by Myron.

459. **Ancient Greek art** was heavily influenced by religion and mythology, with many pieces depicting gods or goddesses.

460. **Greek theater was a popular** form of entertainment during this period. Plays were often performed in open-air amphitheaters built into hillsides.

Ancient Greek Literature

This chapter will explore the captivating world of **ancient Greek literature.** We'll take a look at ten interesting facts about Greek authors, genres, and themes.

461. **Greek literature dates back to the 8ᵗʰ century BCE.**

462. Many genres of literature were popular, including **tragedy, comedy, poetry, and philosophy.**

463. **Ancient Greeks used storytelling** to entertain people during celebrations or festivals like **Dionysia** and **Panathenaea.**

464. **Ancient Greeks believed that gods could take any shape they wanted,** so stories often featured deities turning into animals.

465. **Ancient Greek writers** often wrote about heroes who had to overcome obstacles and go on quests for knowledge or power.

466. **Homer** wrote two of the most famous epic poems in ancient Greece: **the *Iliad*** and **the *Odyssey*.** Historians debate whether Homer was a real person or just a name that has been passed down through the ages.

467. One of the most famous ancient **Greek poets was Sappho,** a woman who was believed to be a princess or the daughter of a wealthy family on **the island of Lesbos.** She wrote her poems from c. 630 to c. 570 BCE).

468. **The philosopher Plato** wrote many famous works, including the ***Republic,*** which talks about his views on justice and governance.

469. **Aristotle's *Poetics*** is still studied today because it gives insight into how some of the earliest plays were formed and how stories should be crafted.

470. Like the artists of today, Greek playwrights had many imitators who would write in the style of **Aeschylus** or **Aristophanes,** for example.

Ancient Greek Language and Alphabet

Explore five interesting facts about **the ancient Greek language and alphabet.** Learn about its twenty-four letters based on phonetic sounds and the letter sigma, which is still being used today in Greece and in math!

471. **The first written form of ancient Greek dates back over three thousand years**. It had a huge influence on many modern languages, including English!

472. **The alphabet used in ancient Greek had twenty-four letters**. There were only capital letters, no lowercase ones! All these letters were based on phonetic sounds, meaning different combinations of them made up each word's sound.

473. **Greek is still considered an essential part of our cultural heritage today.** One special letter in its alphabet is called a **sigma,** which looks like an upside-down horseshoe shape (Σ). It makes a strong double "S" sound.

474. **In addition to being spoken by people living in ancient Greece, it was also widely used throughout the Roman Empire,** especially in education and science. It has been the source of many technical and scientific terms that are still used today.

475. **Greek became the language of the Greek government in 1821** when the Greeks won independence from the Ottoman Turks.

Ancient Greek Warfare

This chapter will explore **the fascinating history of ancient Greek warfare.** We'll look at ten interesting facts about their **tactics, weapons, armor, and siege engines.** We'll also discover how they utilized different **strategies** to outwit their enemies and gain an advantage on **the battlefield**.

476. **The most important Greek battle formation was the phalanx,** which consisted of soldiers standing shoulder to shoulder with long spears pointed outward toward their enemies.

477. **Greek soldiers often used shields** during battles for protection from arrows and other projectiles thrown at them by enemy forces.

478. **Greek warriors used different styles of helmets depending on where they were from.** The most famous of these styles is **the Corinthian style**, which is often seen in movies and TV shows.

479. **Greek helmets usually consisted of a bronze bowl-like** structure with cheek guards attached. They offered excellent protection against sword blows!

480. **Hoplites** were specially trained warriors who fought in heavy armor and carried large shields and spears or swords into battles. They formed the backbone of many ancient Greek armies.

481. **The ancient Greeks had a special unit of soldiers called the peltasts,** who relied on speed and agility rather than armor for protection during battle.

482. **Horseback riding played an essential role in ancient Greek warfare,** especially in the time of Alexander the Great. Mounted warriors could maneuver quickly and attack from unexpected angles.

483. **The Greeks used primitive catapults** to help break down city walls or fortifications that protected enemy forces.

484. Historians still debate **the famous story of the Trojan Horse.** The wooden horse was supposed to be a gift from the Greeks to the Trojans, but it was actually filled with Greek soldiers waiting to attack the Trojans once inside the city.

485. **Many battles involved individual hand-to-hand combat between two sides,** but most battles had large groups clashing all at once.

Ancient Greek Trade and Commerce

This chapter will explore five interesting **facts about ancient Greek trade and commerce.** We'll take a look at their currency, ships, and bartering practices.

486. **Ancient Greek cities had their currencies and coins,** which allowed for trade between different regions, called 'drachma' and used anywhere in the **Mediterranean!**

487. Trade ships were called triremes. They had three banks of oars that could make them very fast in the water!

488. **Merchants from Greece would travel all over the Mediterranean Sea** to trade goods like wine, olive oil, pottery, and jewelry with other civilizations as far away as Egypt and Persia.

489. **The early ancient Greeks traded by bartering.** They exchanged one item for another without using money.

490. **Corinth was one of the most important trading cities in ancient Greece.** Its port was used to send and receive goods from other countries around the Mediterranean.

Ancient Greek Colonization

This chapter will explore **the incredible history of ancient Greek colonization** and its lasting legacy. We'll look at five interesting facts about their **explorations, trading networks,** and how Greek colonization still influences us today!

491. **The ancient Greeks were explorers and settlers.** They sailed in ships across the Mediterranean **to explore new lands and establish colonies,** cities that served as trading hubs for goods like spices and fabrics.

492. **The first Greek colony was established by the city-state of Miletus** in what is now Turkey around 650 BCE. More than five hundred colonies would be founded by ancient Greeks throughout Europe, Asia Minor, North Africa, and even parts of modern-day Russia and Ukraine.

493. **Colonization allowed different cultures to interact with each other,** sometimes peacefully, sometimes not. This exchange led to significant advances in arts, culture, and scientific knowledge.

494. **Greek colonists brought their gods with them.** Their deities became popular among the locals. For example, **Athena was worshiped in many different colonies,** and her statue became a symbol of the colonization process.

495. Most **Greek colonies** were later destroyed or absorbed by the Romans.

Ancient Greek Law and Government

This chapter takes an in-depth look at ancient **Greek law and government.** We will discover five interesting facts about their **legal systems, social classes, and democracy.**

496. The first democratic form of government in the world began in Athens, Greece, around 500 BCE. All citizens had an equal say in how their city-state should be run. Most people were not citizens, though.

497. In ancient Athens, people were divided into three classes: **slaves, free citizens**, and **women.** Slaves had no rights whatsoever. Women had very few rights. Free citizens could usually participate in political decision-making processes, such as voting for leaders or deciding on laws.

498. Trial by jury was common in Greek city-states like Athens during this period. If someone was accused of a crime, they would have their peers decide whether they were innocent or guilty instead of having one person make that decision alone.

499. Greek cities had different legal systems, which varied from region to region. Some, like **Athens** in the Classical Age, were more **liberal** and allowed the people to have a voice. Other city-states, like **Sparta,** were more like **dictatorships.**

500. Ancient Greek philosophers like Socrates, Plato, and Aristotle wrote extensively on politics, ethics, and justice, which greatly influenced later legal systems worldwide.

Conclusion

Ancient Greek civilization has left a lasting legacy that still influences us today. **Its contributions to math, science, art, and literature have shaped our world.** From its **unique alphabet** and language to its **myths of gods and heroes**, ancient Greece was an incredibly influential culture that helped shape history. No wonder it continues to captivate our imagination even thousands of years later!

We are lucky we can **explore this ancient society** through archaeological evidence and written works from **authors like Homer or Plato**, who continue to inspire us with their timeless wisdom. By concluding this journey through **ancient Greece's** past, we can look back on all the incredible achievements made by one of humanity's most **remarkable civilizations**, one whose influence will last for centuries more!

Sources and Additional References

Societies in Transition in Early Greece: An Archaeological History. University of California Press, Oakland, p. 11.

"Visited Releases List of Top 10 Most Popular Ancient Sites." https://www.newswire.com/news/visited-releases-list-of-top-10-most-popular-ancient-sites-21845252.

Finch, Caleb E. The Biology of Human Longevity: Inflammation, Nutrition, and Aging in the Evolution of Lifespans. Amsterdam: Elsevier, 2010.

Amos, Hugh D., and A. G. Lang. These Were the Greeks. Bristol Classical Press, 1996.

Kebric, Robert B. Greek People. McGraw-Hill Humanities Social, 2004.

Pomeroy, Sarah B., Stanley M. Burstein, Walter Donlan, and David W. Tandy. Ancient Greece: A Political, Social, and Cultural History. New York: Oxford University Press, USA, 2017.

Cline, Eric H. The Ancient Greek World: From the Bronze Age to the Death of Alexander the Great. Oxford University Press, 2017.

Murray, Tim. Greek Archaeology: A Guide to Sites and Museums in Greece. University of California Press, 2020.

Carter, Jennifer. Ancient Greece: Everyday Life in the Birthplace of Western Civilization. Scholastic, 2011.

Cartwright, Mark. Ancient Greece: A History from Beginning to End. Hourly History, 2019.

Cartledge, Paul et al., The Spartans: An Epic History, Basic Books, 2003.

Finley, M. I., and Oswyn Murray, eds. The Oxford History of the Classical World: Greece and the Hellenistic World (Oxford University Press, 1986).

Rowlandson, Jane and Christopher Rowe Eds. Greek Philosophers: Socrates to Aristotle (Routledge Classics 2001).

Kagan, Donald. The Peloponnesian War. Penguin Books, 2003.

Herodotus. The Histories. Translated by Aubrey de Selincourt (New York: Penguin Books, 1972).

Cartledge, Paul. Alexander the Great: The Hunt for a New Past. Macmillan, 2004.

Check out another book in the series